IN A VERY ENGLISH TOWN

IN A VERY ENGLISH TOWN

Photographs at Thame, Oxfordshire, 2007-2008

John Comino-James

dewi lewis publishing

IN A VERY ENGLISH TOWN
BY JOHN COMINO-JAMES

First published in the United Kingdom in 2009 by

Dewi Lewis Publishing
8 Broomfield Road, Heaton Moor
Stockport SK4 4ND, England
www.dewilewispublishing.com

The author acknowledges the following as sources of reference and quotation:
A History of Thame, J Howard Brown & William Guest, 1935
An Innkeeper's Diary and *My Three Inns,* John Fothergill, Chatto & Windus, 1931 & 1951
Thame Inns Discovered, Allan Hickman & David Bretherton, Daal Publishing, 2000

ISBN: 978-1-904587-72-9

Design and Layout: Dewi Lewis Publishing
Print: EBS, Verona, Italy

previous page: Parish Church of St Mary the Virgin, July 2007

IN A VERY ENGLISH TOWN

These photographs were made in response to an invitation from a Cuban friend to make and show her some photographs of my local town, Thame, which lies just north of the Chiltern Hills, some forty-five miles from London. The majority were made between July 2007 and February 2008. The last was made in June 2008. They are not presented chronologically but in a more or less geographical sequence, suggesting a progress through a town whose central layout was established to facilitate commerce in the Middle Ages.

This journey, marked by particular landmarks and various encounters, passes through streets whose names – Buttermarket, Cornmarket, Pump Lane, North Street, Park Street – have such a deceptive familiarity to the English ear that they might be expected to recur in almost any town in England.

Although the population has grown considerably in the last thirty years, most of the residential and industrial development has taken place within reach of but away from the heart of the town. No retail park has been built on its outskirts. Moreover, the few streets where these photographs were made have been largely spared the more excessive depredations of developers in the same period. In a townscape that has evolved over time buildings from different periods sit more or less comfortably one with another and offer a reassuring sense of continuity. The varying heights and the different architectural styles create a pleasant and uneven skyline which draws the eye upwards without restraint. For the most part, however, these photographs quite deliberately avoid this expanded view, presenting instead a direct framing of the frontages or of exchanges in the street.

While the inevitable and necessary presence of High Street chain stores, supermarkets, charity shops, and services such as banks, travel agents and estate agents is acknowledged, closer attention is paid to the present day weekly markets and annual fairs which are the descendants of those which led to the expansion of the town in the 13th century. More particularly, formal portraits introduce some of those independent shopkeepers whose collective aim might be summed up in the words of one of them: *"To keep the character of Thame as a Market Town and not a Supermarket town".*

JOHN COMINO-JAMES

Priest End, August 2007

High Street, April 2008

High Street, April 2008

Brook Lane (Cuttlebrook House and The Six Bells, High Street), April 2008

The Forge, High Street, March 2008

When you speak of history, a lot of the ironwork round here has R R Timms stamped on it somewhere. Ralph Timms came here in the 1920s. In his book, *An Innkeeper's Diary*, John Fothergill mentions that Ralph was altering his grand-father's work when he added to the metalwork of the sign at the Spread Eagle. Ralph and his son Rupert also made the church gates. Just recently I renovated some gates which I would say were made here back in the 1950s, an absolutely superb bit of work. The only repairs that needed doing were where four of the centre scrolls needed to be taken out because rust had got behind them and blown them apart. They needed remaking and refitting, which is what I did. Those gates are absolutely stunning. They would cost thousands to reproduce these days, a beautiful bit of work, all banded, collared, riveted through the frame, superb.

Rupert was still here when we bought the house in 1979 – they were still shoeing horses here in the early 1980s. By the time we'd done up the house I decided it would be a shame to convert the forge into a lounge or something like that and I thought I'd just take it up as a hobby and that's how it all started really. I'd never done it before. I went to a six-evening course at Rycotewood College, which of course has now closed. It was pretty basic really, they just told you how to make a poker.

My son Zeke works with me. At the moment we've got an enormous fruit garden enclosure on the go for Rycote Park. That's about 70 feet by 20 feet with three gates into it all covered in mesh.

Probably the most interesting work that we do comes about when people are renovating listed buildings. You can't buy anything off the shelf which will satisfy the listed building people so it has to be made in exactly the same way as it was a couple of hundred years ago. You can only do that with a forge and starting from scratch with the steel. Heat and beat.

From a conversation with David Moss, July 2008

David Moss, The Forge, High Street, July 2007

High Street, April 2008

High Street, July 2007

Thame Tandoori, High Street, April 2008

High Street, August 2007

Mia Capri, High Street, July 2007

We opened here in October 2005. The idea behind this shop was to focus on the Fair Trade side of things which now accounts for about 80% of what we sell. That includes a range of incense, clothing, textiles, and really beautiful jewellery.

I love doing what I do, I like being surrounded by beautiful things, I like spreading the joy and being able to do something that helps other people as well is just fantastic.

Fair Trade actually means the people who make the items I sell get paid a proper wage. They're usually paid in advance, paid at order so they don't have to go into debt in order to make their products, so therefore it's like getting a regular income, a regular wage, and they can plan ahead, whereas before it was very much a hand to mouth existence and they didn't know where the next money was coming from and so they couldn't plan ahead very much.

My ethos behind the whole shop is that doing the Fair Trade side of things is my way of making a contribution, I can't change the world but I can change this bit of it. I can't make a difference with the rest of it but I can make a difference here.

From a conversation with Claire Hewison-Billsborough, March 2008

Claire Hewison-Billsborough, Sapphire Moon, High Street, March 2008

It's called Buddies because that's what we are, best friends as well as business partners. We couldn't call it 'Friends' because of the association with the TV programme, so it became Buddies.

Plus we liked playing on the word in our menu, Buddies Basics, Buddie Busta, Buddie Breakfast Box, Buddie Good, and so on.

We opened in February 2002. And of course when we began we thought just the two of us would be able to do it, but on the first day we were so busy we thought, What have we started!

From a conversation with Sandra Tipping, July 2008

Sandra Tipping and Nicky Priest, Buddies Breakfast and Sandwich Bar, High Street, November 2007

Buddies Breakfast and Sandwich Bar, High Street, October 2007

Every town needs a bookshop – it is the lifeblood of a thriving community.

The Book House has been established in Thame for over thirty five years. It began when my former business partner opened one of the first children's bookshops in the country as The Red House. It was sited in the Lower High Street in a beautiful red brick house, which was for a time the home of W B Yeats. My business partner and I worked together for 10 years and during that time we opened a second shop in Summertown, Oxford; moved the Thame shop to its present site and started a successful book club which operated from the Tithe Barn close to St Mary's church. I've owned the business since 1983 and have re-established The Book House as a family bookshop with a strong emphasis on children's books – a passion we will never lose.

We probably carry something like 20,000 titles in stock, but we have access to over 300,00 titles from wholesalers on a 24 hour basis. We use that service all the time. Of course we pay for it, but it keeps us alive on the High Street. If we order a book by 4.00 pm one day, it will be here by 9.30 am the next morning and, moreover, we can tell which books are being sent to us before they arrive.

Until about ten years ago the Net Book Agreement forbade booksellers to sell books cheaper than the published price. That was brilliant, because although the bookselling chains might get more discount they couldn't sell books cheaper than we could and so competition was based alone on knowledge and quality of service. But when the Net Book Agreement was abolished then even supermarkets could sell books as they sell yoghurt, as they sell frozen peas: simply as merchandise.

And, of course, there's now Amazon. They are stiff competition because they don't have to go into a High Street situation and pay High Street rents or rates or pay booksellers who have a real love and knowledge and interest in books. I mean we have booksellers who've been with us for more than twenty five years who know books inside out and upside-down.

People might very well go into their local bookshop to see a book and then go to Amazon to try and buy that same book cheaper, but in the end their local town is the loser because if that independent bookseller closes then there's no way for people to inspect books, to come in to browse ... and who can deny the joy of quiet moments spent browsing in a bookshop?

From a conversation with Brian Pattinson, March 2008

Brian Pattinson, The Bookhouse, High Street, July 2007

I took over here in May 2007.

We offer a personal service so coming to Elegance is not just a shopping trip, it's a whole experience.

Customers often come looking for guidance and we are all too aware that someone coming in can be feeling quite vulnerable about their body image. We want them to go out feeling special, that they've rediscovered their elegance. When that happens we know we've really done our job. That's what we're here for.

From a conversation with Patricia Wright, July 2008

Patricia Wright, Elegance of Thame Ltd., High Street, January 2008

Togs 4 U, The Masonic Hall, and Buckell & Ballard, High Street, June 2008

Elegance of Thame Ltd., Thame House Dental Practice, and Browns Solicitors, High Street, November 2007

High Street, August 2007

I tend to take a back seat while my sons run the business but I do like to be in touch with the public.

When I first started in business people were having large joints, traditional roasts; now people tend to want it all finely prepared. It comes down to a different way of presenting meat to the customer. We need volume in the business, so as well as traditional meat and poultry we produce a lot of pies. We are now making several thousand pies a week for Budgens.

It's very important that meat comes from animals that are properly fed and handled. We try to specialise in free-range poultry. We buy a lot of our beef in Scotland, the pastures are good. Over the years you get to know the people who are feeding cattle well. We deal with a man who is a generous feeder, feeding swedes and turnips and barley. You get moisture in the meat, you get good meat. When cattle are fed on beans you get hard meat. How a beast is slaughtered is important too. Cattle can tense you see, which affects the meat. An animal should die happy and without stress. A lot of meat sold is killed on a Monday and in a box on a Thursday. We don't operate like that. We hang our beef for ten days. There's also too much emphasis placed on lean meat. For the flavour you need a little bit of fat in the meat, like the marbling.

I remember when there were six butchers in Thame. Now there are two. Our business is growing and I'm certain it's because of our quality. We have very discerning customers and I'm very fussy about what we have in the shop.

From a conversation with Michael Newitt, July 2008

Michael Newitt, M. Newitt & Sons, High Street, June 2008

Plaque commemorating the site of the Girls' Grammar School, High Street, August 2007

High Street, July 2007

We are an independent company with our head office in Chesham and branches in Maidenhead and Beaconsfield as well as here in Thame.

We stock a variety of washing machines, tumble dryers, dishwashers, fridges, freezers and freestanding cookers. You can see that we also carry a large range of small appliances like vacuum cleaners, food processors, irons, kettles, toasters and so on.

Whilst it would be fair to say that trading times have changed radically over the last few years, there is still a need for a company like ours in the High Street; after all not everybody's got a car and not everybody wants to go out to a retail park.

Of course we face competition from the Internet. We class ourselves as 'bricks', as in bricks and mortar: our competitors selling over the internet are 'clicks'. A lot of business does go to clicks, and a lot of younger people shop on-line. We compete because we can offer fast and free delivery within a reasonable distance, free connection of all free-standing products and free disposal of old equipment with the exclusion of refrigeration which is now the responsibility of County Councils. We subscribe to the WEE – Waste Electrical and Electronic Equipment – Directive; redundant washing machines, cookers, dishwashers – all our major stock items – will go back for recycling.

We can resolve any installation problems that the customers may have either directly or indirectly. The amount of people that come into us on a Saturday afternoon because they've had a product delivered and find that they can't connect it for one reason or another is quite staggering. We'll advise them but we'll also tell them that if they'd bought from us in the first place they wouldn't have had that problem. I have a light-hearted saying, If you've bought it elsewhere we've both lost money.

From a conversation with Tony Herbert, April 2008

Tony Herbert, Domesco Ltd., High Street, July 2007

Woolworths, Lightfoots, and Martin's, High Street, September 2007

Nationwide, The Co-operative Travel, and Autoparts, High Street, October 2007

High Street, August 2007

… In the summer of 1924 I wrote to the Council asking permission to put the sign up on a post on the pavement, which they wouldn't have had power to do had I not told them that it would take the place of an ugly lamp-post which I would light at my own expense. The Council came in force to interview me on a summer evening at eight o'clock outside the house when dinner was in full swing, and I was in a white duck dress-suit, and it began to drizzle. I was given permission and a chill.

… When he saw it up, Mr. Robinson, the surveyor, was very nervous as 'it was a much bigger thing than the Council ever anticipated,' which 'was more like this,' he said, kicking a scaffold pole. 'What,' he asked, 'would they do if every publican and eating-house in Thame asks to put up a sign?' I told him that if they could find lamp-posts to replace signs with, it would be much to the good.

Extracts from John Fothergill, My Three Inns

Eagle Antiques & Curios and The Spread Eagle Hotel, Cornmarket, April 2008

The High Street has changed drastically over the last twenty years, I mean drastically, not just a bit.

We've lost shops that I personally think were a real benefit to the town. Shops like Potters the ironmongers, Imps which sold clothes, Freeman Hardy and Willis, the wool shop down in North Street. Pied Pedaller will be going. I could make quite a list. We used to have three chemists, now we've got one. There's no greengrocer as such. The Post Office has gone into Martin's the newsagents, and the one in Park Street has closed down altogether. Like most towns we've seen more services coming in, and more Charity shops. There's a place for them but they don't have the costs that an ordinary shop has to carry.

It is getting harder for the independent retailer with just one shop. I think the Internet is the biggest infringement on the High Street today. I've got friends who buy almost everything off the Internet. They hardly need to come to the town at all. Yet to me the most important thing about shopping or having a shop is the dealing with people. In 1971 I started Petcare, which is now next door, and I know from experience that people like to see you behind the till, managing the shop. I used to say to my staff that without that customer at the till buying their 5p dogchew or whatever, they didn't have a job. How many times have you left a shop without so much as a thank-you or goodbye?

At one time Thame had a lot of antique shops, now I'm the only one.

I want to work till I'm 80 if I can because I love working and I love meeting people and doing bits and pieces but it is changing big time at the moment and sometimes it looks as if there won't be any antique trade. But there again in a few years time it might revert back.

From a conversation with Terry Guest, February 2008

Terry Guest, Eagle Antiques & Curios, Cornmarket, July 2007

People want clean, modern shopping, they want to see everything nice and clean, with stainless steel cages and glass cabinets. The old fashioned dingy pet shop wouldn't survive anymore. So what I try to do is to look at other retailers – not necessarily pet shops – and see how they market themselves, how they display things.

We keep small mammals like rabbits, hamsters, chinchillas, gerbils and rats. We sell finches and parakeets though not so many parrots – that market's much quieter now. We also do small things like stick insects and axolotls which are more for children's bedrooms really. But for all the animals we sell, we offer also an after sales hotel facility. So if you buy a rabbit from us and go away on holiday you can bring it back and we'll look after it here and charge a daily rate. It's an after sales service so that people can feel confident that they can take on a small pet and still go away on holiday and know it's being looked after properly.

We stock tropical and cold water fish, and we also install aquariums in companies' premises or in people's houses and we go back to service and maintain them.

We have a whole array of toys and food and accessories for pets.

And then we've got back to where the business originally started, delivering pet food. People want to buy locally and they want home deliveries again so we do a Friday run to all the villages.

Besides all that, the Internet is another opportunity. Without it we wouldn't be the business we are. I can't see how a modern business can survive without it. It's another form of High Street. We don't open on a Sunday but we're still taking money. On a Monday morning we could have another 20 sales through the web site. And we didn't even open the doors to do that.

From a conversation with Jason Nicholls, April 2008

Jason Nicholls, Petcare, Cornmarket, July 2007

Peter Mullen, The Money Spinner Ltd., Cornmarket, March 2008

Oxfam Bookshop, Cornmarket, December 2007

Abingdon Arms, Robert Stanley Opticians, and Woolworths, Cornmarket, November 2007

Parkers and Thame Trading Co., Cornmarket, November 2007

We started in October 2005 so we've been going for about two and half years. The principal idea is to offer handmade food just as you'd produce at home but for people who perhaps haven't got time to do it themselves. We source our ingredients very carefully. We use local products if we can, not necessarily organic but good quality.

I like to think people come to me because they know I cook the products myself and they know they are made in the way that they would make them at home. Have a look at my cooker there, I'm just using regulation saucepans and I'm making very small batches.

We have customers who bring in their own dishes and we fill them up with things for dinner parties and so on. We also do quite a lot of outside catering, lunches for boardroom meetings, food for weddings and funerals.

I think many people have got so used to shopping for everything in supermarkets that they don't really explore the town. I thought this was a good location here in Cornmarket, a corner plot, nice big windows but the footfall going past is not what you'd think it would be. Unless people are going to the bank there's no real reason for them to come through this part of the town. A lot of people park in Waitrose, they come up Greyhound Walk and they either go right or they go left and miss us out. I think there's a lot more footfall in the Buttermarket than there is here.

At the end of the day I want to do something that I enjoy doing as a living. I'm passionate about food and cooking is what really interests me so I'm trying to develop a career or a business in which I can enjoy myself.

From a conversation with Tony Hazelton, March 2008

Tony Hazelton, Sally Dickinson, and Liz Gunn, What's Cooking?, Cornmarket, November 2007

Steamer Trading Cookshop, Robert Gatward, and Tim Russ & Company, High Street, July 2007

High Street, August 2007

High Street, July 2007

High Street, August 2007

Austins, High Street, December 2007

George, Big Issue seller, Greyhound Walk, August 2007

John Hampden Memorial and preparations for Remembrance Day Parade, High Street, 11 November 2007

We've been here eleven years, from February 1997, plus before that I'd been working here for two years as the manager of the previous business, De Gustibus. So I've been here for 13 years altogether.

We are one of the few Italian food specialists left in the country selling just Italian food products and nothing else. Most of our produce comes direct from Italy, and where the mass-market stops we start. For instance you can buy many kinds of pasta in the supermarket but the pasta we sell is made by small producers who don't produce for the mass market. Our olives all come from different regions in Italy. They all come in brine and the art is to make the dressing. I experiment with dressing all the time, I say I can make a hundred kinds but I can do more than that, no problem! My passion is cooking and Italian food, it's obvious! If I lose that passion, the shop will die!

From a conversation with Umberto Della Valle, March 2008

Umberto Della Valle, Umberto's. Greyhound Walk, February 2008

I love food but I didn't like what I saw as being done to our food with chemicals right through the whole process. However when I used to go to Health shops I found them really quite intimidating; I just thought it was almost like a niche market whereas I felt it should be open to everyone. So for a while I wanted to get into this and now we're in our 6th year here. We've opened a second shop in Amersham which my husband runs.

When we first started there seemed to be a lot less general information available unless you were a vegetarian or a vegan or had particular dietary needs. But now, for whatever reason, things like gluten and wheat free or dairy and yeast free foods are becoming a daily requirement for more and more people. And more and more people are interested in dietary supplements. I sometimes think we're kind of pioneers, we promote and inform and then it all goes mainstream and the supermarkets get involved. Sometimes that's frustrating because it feels as if we've done all the hard work but then on the plus side it's making people healthier and more informed and educated.

Besides the supplements and the food side of the business we find people are also thinking more about the content of the skincare products they use, so natural, paraben-free toiletries are a growth area for us. We also sell the Ecover household range of household products, but with the difference that we offer a refill service for the laundry liquids. I see that as a way of reducing the amount of plastic that would otherwise be thrown away.

I like to inform people and to advise people; I like to think that even if people come in and don't buy anything they might be a little more aware when they leave the door. As long as I make enough money to survive!

From a conversation with Suzy Dewdney, April 2008

Jo Cherry and Suzy Dewdney, Planet Health and Organics, Greyhound Walk, February 2008

Waitrose, Greyhound Lane, September 2007

This site is owned by South Oxfordshire District Council and the business is now owned by a farmer's cooperative, Thame Farmers Auction Mart Ltd. We've just now got planning permission for a new market up at the Showground.

At the time the Cattle Market moved here in 1951 there were still other markets at Slough, Tring, Winslow, Leigton Buzzard, Olney, Northampton, Bedford, Banbury, and down as far as Guildford. Now only Winslow and Thame remain.

Thame market was always held on a Tuesday, but now the two auction days are Wednesday and Friday. Those are the traditional Aylesbury days, Wednesday for prime stock and Friday for store stock. On a Friday now we could be selling cattle for farmers from anywhere in the local area right the way down to Brighton, Southampton even down into Kent. We now have a big catchment area.

I think they say that you don't train to be an auctioneer, especially not a livestock auctioneer, but that you're born to it. You've got to have that ability, the flair to perform. It's a bit like being a singer or an actor going on stage, you're playing a role.

You're building a trade and you need to create a momentum and keep it going. Our job is to make as much for the vendor as possible because we work for the vendor. You practice your speech just as an actor would, you talk to yourself and get your ability to roll the words. It only comes with practice. And the other thing is you've got to have a good eye for stock and you've got to have a good eye for valuation. Every lot that comes in you instantly value. And that again comes with practice and experience.

Three people go to an auction, one who goes to sell, one who goes to buy and one who goes to watch. The one who's watching could be a buyer or seller another day. You have to perform for all three, you have to make the vendor feel that you've worked for him and you've still got to make the buyer feel that he's important and that he's bought his animal at a good price. It's a fine line. It's good fun. The adrenaline gets going and you get a real kick out of it.

From a conversation with Simon Draper, July 2008

Sale Ring, Thame Farmers Auction Mart Ltd., North Street, April 2008

Martin Foster, Thame Farmers Auction Mart Ltd., North Street, February 2008

Simon Draper, Principal Auctioneer, and Sandy Young, Thame Farmers Auction Mart Ltd., North Street, April 2008

Craft 'T' Sue's, North Street, April 2008

Ciao Baby and The Chocolate Box, North Street, August 2007

I collect rugs myself. I mean I love rugs. I was born in a town that is very famous for rug making so that actually influenced me in getting the knowledge of the business. And of course my parents and my grandparents always loved rugs. You know it is in our blood to love rugs.

We know the artists when we buy Persian rugs. The thing is that when you are a business your door is always open, you have to be a hundred percent sure that the customer will be satisfied. So we pick the best and we get the best for people and we give the best, simple as that, we don't have any problems and they don't have any problems... And these rugs never lose their value.

Think about it, it's like painting: as the mentality of the artist changes the work changes as well, the colour changes, and his age, his maturity changes his rug-making as well.

If an artist made a rug twenty years ago and then you go and you see his work now it will be completely different. What you will see is the development of the type of work he has done. It's going to be lighter, it's going to be a tighter knot, it's going to be in some way completely different work. The maturity, straight away, is going to hit you.

You can move to a new house but when you drop a rug that you love onto the floor then it's your house because you have just put your sign there without any effort. You put what you love there and you will always love it and you will take it with you when you leave.

From a conversation with Emad Razavi, February 2008

Emad Razavi, Tapis, North Street, December 2007

We like to offer a personal traditional service which means everything that any gentleman's hairdresser would offer apart from shaving. Basically there's not a lot of call for shaving these days.

A few years ago I could have told you exactly which days would be quieter or which would be busier but more recently it's so up and down you just don't know. I think the whole pattern of everything's changed. Although we don't work on Sundays there are a lot of places that do, and some supermarkets are open 24 hours. Perhaps we get more shift workers than we did before. It all makes a difference. Perhaps over the next few years a new pattern will emerge. The business has been here about eighty odd years and I've owned it since 1986 though I did work here for a little while before that.

I started as an apprentice in 1966 in High Wycombe at a shop called Peters. The apprenticeship was three years and I did two more years to become fully qualified. I worked there for a few years and when they opened another shop I went on to manage that. When that was taken over I stayed on for a while before moving to another place in Wycombe for a year. Then I came here. When I come to look back I realise I've only ever worked in four different establishments in forty two years.

But even when the time comes for me to finish here I can't see myself stopping completely. I'll still be involved in hairdressing in some way because I really enjoy what I do.

From a conversation with Ian Lee, April 2008

Ian Lee, Thame Hair, North Street, November 2007

Pied Pedaller, North Street, December 2007

Malcolm Kew, Kew Bookbinding, North Street, December 2007

The Cutting Rooms, Buttermarket, July 2007

Haircut for charity, Buttermarket, July 2007

Matthew Cundy, Kismet Jewellers, Buttermarket, August 2007

Buttermarket, April 2008

Buttermarket, August 2007

Fore Golf, Buttermarket, July 2007

Pump Lane (Brothers and Thomson Travel, Buttermarket), November 2007

Obviously people come in to meet friends; in a way it's one of the things we're here for. But one day when I came in one of the girls came up to me and said, "They're interviewing on table 11." I left it a while and went up and asked them how it was going and they said "Oh we're interviewing for the new café opening up down the road." "Oh!" I said, "You come in my café to interview for that!"

OK, fine, as I say there's enough room for another cafe, it doesn't worry me from that point of view but after a while I went back and said "Look guys I really need the table, it's getting near lunchtime," so I moved them into the back restaurant and their interviewees kept coming in all day long. Eventually they had some coffee and then they turned round and said to the girl who was serving them and said, "That coffee was absolute rubbish," and told her go down and try their coffee sometime.

As it happened, when they did open I didn't think their coffee was as good as ours.

But I did get a bit upset about that.

From a conversation with Robert Dowden, March 2008

Robert Dowden, The Coffee Shop, Buttermarket, February 2008

I'm a Chartered Surveyor and Estate Agent and I now specialise in commercial property. I deal mostly with shops, offices, and factories in Thame and the surrounding villages. I get involved not only with sales but lettings, rent reviews, lease renewal negotiations as well as surveys, and general surveying and planning work.

We've seen an increase in barn conversions, not simply to housing but also to offices because farmers have been encouraged to diversify and in some cases have been able to obtain small grants to convert barns into offices. I've been involved in letting those, which I've found an enjoyable part of my business. I enjoy dealing with business people. I find it stimulating to be involved in their relocation plans and finding the kind of premises they require and following that through.

I have a love for buildings, especially old buildings. I'm the son of an architect and I was lucky to have been encouraged from an early age to respect buildings and to enjoy their architecture and their use.

I've seen the town grow, though more residentially than commercially. It's retained its character largely because the town centre is predominantly listed buildings and is very protected by planning law. There's been a limit to the amount of new shops though, of course, we have them in Swan Walk and also in Greyhound Walk, the shopping development leading to Waitrose.

I enjoy letting offices to young companies, perhaps someone who's been working from home moves into a small office, perhaps two or three rooms above a shop, then two or three years later I find them something larger as they expand and employ more staff. I've watched them move on, and I'll have had the phone call from them saying they need to move into larger premises now, can I find them something larger.

I speak to and meet new people every day and I think it's the meeting people that's so enjoyable, finding out about their business, about what their requirements are in property and showing them round properties, helping them to secure the right property for their business to grow into. I don't think I'll ever get tired of that. It gets in your system, doesn't it, it's your career, your employment, it's what you do, what you think. It's a part of who you are.

From a conversation with Stephen Humpston, February 2008

Stephen Humpston, Honour & Company, High Street, February 2008

I started ThameNews.Net in January 2003, and acquired the sister website Thame.Net the following year.

Thame.Net has been in existence for about eleven years. It's a website with information about Thame, the history of Thame, where to eat, where to stay and so on. It's got information about local groups and churches, about bus timetables, trains and there's also a business and services directory of over 200 local businesses which is categorised so that if anyone wants a builder or a printer or a wedding planner they can look and find a local service. The emphasis is on all things local and we try to support the local economy and encourage people to use local services.

ThameNews.Net aims to meet a different need. It's basically an online daily newspaper for Thame and the surrounding area. It's available either by subscription or simply by looking on the web. The advantage of the subscription is that every weekday all subscribers receive a list of news headlines as an email message and each of those headlines is a link to the relevant page on the website. Subscribers can tell at once if there is a news item of interest to them. The alternative is to remember to log on to the website and hunt around in all the different sections to see if there's any news, any sports, any entertainments of interest. People like to use it in different ways really.

I started it because I had come to realise that one of the problems with a traditional weekly paper published on a Friday is that if anything happens on a Thursday or Friday it doesn't appear till the following week by which time it's old news. Our strap-line is 'Local News as it Happens'. So if I go to a planning meeting on a Tuesday night and there's a controversial planning decision then in theory I can go home and put the result on the website straight away.

From a conversation with Sonja Francis, March 2008

Sonja Francis, ThameNews.Net, Buttermarket, November 2007

Old Nags Head and Gallery Hadley, Upper High Street, September 2007

Entrance to Swan Walk, Upper High Street, August 2007

In the old days somebody would come in and ask you questions and then they'd buy from you. These days they'll ask you questions and then go and buy elsewhere. Ok you've just seen the gentleman there, he may be back, he may not. The price I've quoted him is no different to the likes of John Lewis or anybody else but he might now decide to go and look on the Internet and see if he can find it cheaper …

That said, I certainly think the old saying that people buy from people is very, very true. To me, every single customer who comes through that door is a special customer and I don't care whether he spends £1 or £10,000 he's entitled to the same degree of respect. But that's just me.

From a conversation with Steve Algar, November 2007

Steve Algar, Thame AV, Swan Walk, August 2007

I do still, even after fourteen years, get a buzz at the change of season with all the exciting new colours, the new fabrics, the new designs and everyone coming in to look. Parents who like to have things that are different for their children are always enthusiastic about the new stock, they've got bored with the previous season's and they want to see what's exciting and new.

The art is in putting the things together. Because I buy all my own stock, I know exactly what I've got really well. A mum may pick a pair of trousers or a skirt but then I'll suggest a top or a tee-shirt or a cardigan that will make it look even better. And it's great to have a little one come in and try something on and love it so much they want to leave in it.

From a conversation with Trisha Morrison, February 2008

Trisha Morrison, Charlotte's Web, Swan Walk, February 2008

Arts Desire, Swan Walk, February 2008

Chris Whitmore, Postman, Swan Walk, September 2007

Amanda Beaumont, Key Miniatures, Swan Walk, March 2008

Swan Walk, April 2008

Karen Lumpkin, Vicky Burrows, Adam King, George Rumsey, Rumsey's Chocolaterie, Upper High Street, July 2007

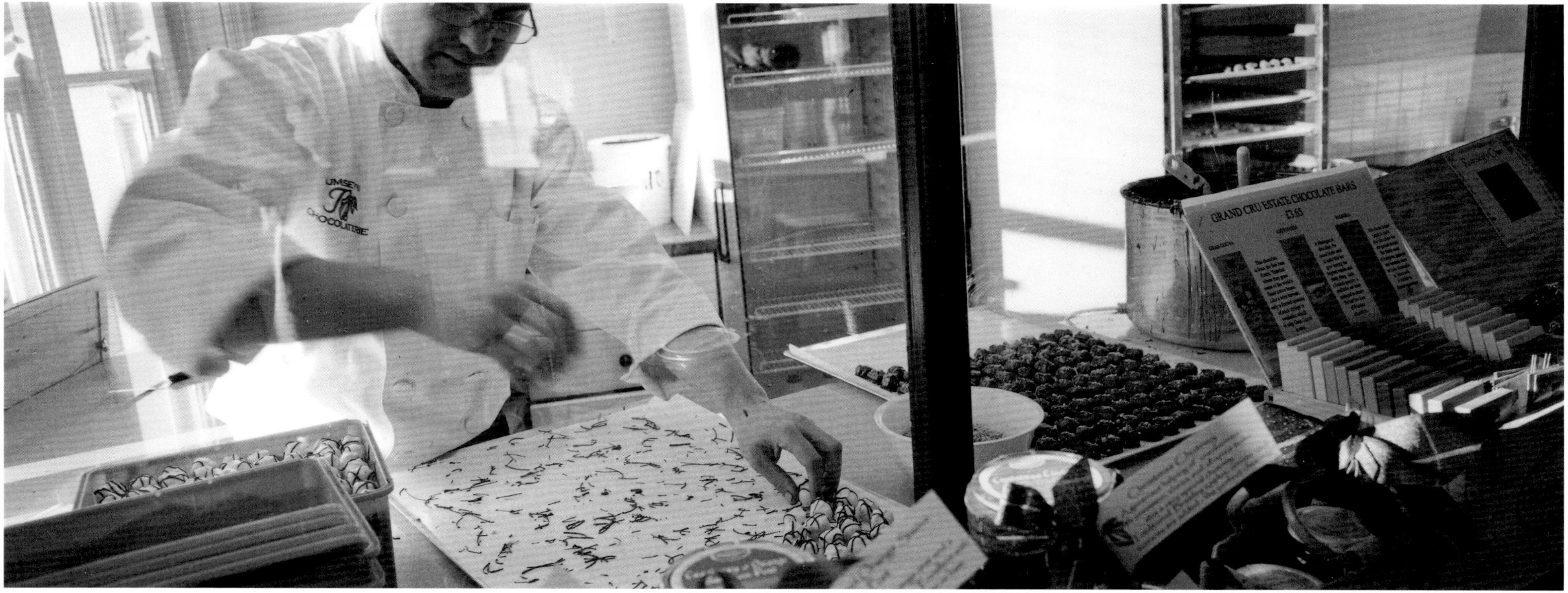

Pavel, Rumsey's Chocolaterie, Upper High Street, December 2007

The hardest thing, emotionally, was to take the decision to close the business. After seven years here that was very hard indeed.

Now in a way is the easy part, it's just a matter of selling as much of the stock as possible.

The next really hard thing will be the day I lock the door for the last time and hand back the keys.

From a conversation with Adrian Mills, February 2008

Mi Casa, Upper High Street, February 2008

Mi Casa and Greens Furnishings, Upper High Street, August 2007

Shoecare and Helen & Douglas House, Upper High Street, June 2008

Our grandfather used to have a shop selling furniture and beds where Boots is now. Dad worked there for a few years, but he decided he didn't enjoy working for somebody else. So he set up by himself. Mum and Dad began in 1963 in a very small shop beyond where 'A Piece of Cake' is now.

That's how it all started. Work was always coming home and that's basically how we got involved. That was how out of choice or out of direction we ended up in the family business.

Every school holiday we were either fitting carpets or delivering furniture or fitting curtains. It's always been our life. Dad thought it best for us to get a bit of retail experience and we worked at Debenhams for a couple of years as training. We also went to London to do a year's college.

We primarily do soft furnishings, carpets, curtains, and upholstery. We've now ventured into haberdashery because the knitting shop in North Street closed three or four years ago. It is something that goes with our trade, it brings people into the shop and we also felt it was something that the town needed so we did that.

Even though father passed away last year it used to give him great pleasure to walk up and down the High Street and see Greens still here and his two boys still running the business he started.

From a conversation with Peter and Tim Green, March 2008

Peter and Tim Green, Greens Furnishings, Upper High Street, February 2008

Shoecare, Upper High Street, November 2007

Richard Webb, Upper High Street, July 2007

Car Park, Upper High Street, November 2007

Following the removal of the Cattle Market from Upper High Street to the North Street site in 1951, the retail market moved from Cornmarket to its present position in the Upper High Street.

The rights to hold both markets and fairs were confirmed in a Royal Charter in 1215: *'in recompense also of robberies, injuries and damages done to the Church of the Blessed Mary of Lincoln, and to the Venerable Father Hugh, Bishop of Lincoln the Second, in the time of the general interdict,'* King John gave, granted and confirmed ... *'that the aforesaid Bishop and his successors shall have Fairs every year to endure three or four days, and Markets every week for one day, throughout all their manors, when and where they shall please and be able to have them without injury of neighbouring fairs and markets appertaining.'*

In the Middle Ages weekly markets provided for the sale and purchase of local produce and were located so that it would be possible for people from the surrounding area to make the return journey to market within the hours of daylight. The primary purpose of the old fairs was also trade, often providing an opportunity for the sale of goods beyond those available at the weekly market.

The stated purpose of the old fairs seems to have been quite specific although probably not exclusive. In *A Genuine and Authentic Account of all the fairs in England and Wales* compiled and published in 1762 *'by the King's Authority'*, William Owen mentions Thame Easter Tuesday *'for all sorts of cattle'* and Thame old Michaelmas October 10th *'for hiring servants, horses, and fat hogs'.* Elsewhere he mentions Bampton August 26 *'for horses and toys'*, Bicester August 5 *'for tanned leather and horses'* and Burford July 5 *'for horses, sheep, cows, and small ware'* and Sept 25 *'for cheese and toys'.*

Richard Cowles, Thame Market, July 2007

Market Fun Day, Thame Market, August 2007

Chris Hurdman and Nick Nicosia, Thame Market, July 2007

Mike Broun's Egg Stall, Thame Market, July 2007

Royal British Legion Poppy Appeal, Thame Market, October 2007

Garden ornaments, Thame Market, December 2007

Terry Hankins, Thame Market, July 2007

Of the two fairs now held in the town under the auspices of The Showmen's Guild it is The Charter, Michaelmas, or October Fair which is a survival from the granting of a Royal Charter in 1215 by King John to the Bishop Hugh Troteman of Lincoln.

Writing in *World's Fair* in 1957, Harry Godfrey referred to the passing of the old customs of hiring and horse-dealing and noted that a well-known Bicester dealer had brought the last horses to the fair some nine years previously. Speaking of the Charter Fair in 1997 the Showman George Rawlins enthused: *'All over there at the back by the Swan used to be roped off. Oh, it used to be lovely they used to run the horses from there to there and run them back and somebody'ld make a bid. I used to love it.'*

Thame Show Fair is organisationally entirely separate from the one day agricultural show which has its origins in a ploughing match held in 1855. Though still referred to locally as Thame Show, this event was renamed The Oxfordshire County & Thame Show in 2006. The Fair commences on Show Day, the third Thursday of September, and lasts for three days.

The Charter Fair is confined to the car park in the Upper High Street. The Show Fair stretches almost from Bell Lane to the Memorial Gardens occupying the High Street, Cornmarket and Upper High Street.

Ray Pearson, Thame Show Fair, September 2007

David Dodds, Bill Pettigrove, Jenny Dodds, Thame Show Fair, September 2007

Dolphe Crick, Thame Show Fair, September 2007

Jozef, Edvard, Jan, Tibor and Miro, Slovak workmen, Upper High Street, February 2008

Fire Services Benevolent Fund charity car wash, Upper High Street, March 2008

Russell Atalay, Thame Kebab, Upper High Street, August 2007

Upper High Street, July 2007

Upper High Street, July 2007

The Aga Shop and The Chippy, Upper High Street, August 2007

Upper High Street, June 2008

Peggy Long, Traffic Warden, Upper High Street, October 2007

Chris Bowler, Upper High Street, October 2007

We sell cake decorating equipment and supplies.

We started in 1985 when we were both doing cake decorating classes. There was nowhere to buy the equipment so we decided to start up so that anyone attending local classes would have somewhere to buy what they needed.

A lot of local people just think we do cakes, they don't realise we sell equipment and that we send it off all over the place. The major part of our business is mail order. We've done orders today for Turkey and Australia. We've got a website too. It's just a little shop in a little town yet here we are, people know us all over the world. Yet to begin with we had to spread our stock around to make it look as if we had anything at all.

In the UK it's evening classes that promote a lot of our business. A lot of the tutors up and down the country know about us and they'll tell their students. We always know when courses begin. We can usually tell what's being demonstrated and taught and where, who's doing bluebells in Birmingham and who's doing cyclamen in Devon, that sort of thing.

From a conversation with Norma Laver and Jenny Walker, February 2008

Jenny Walker and Norma Laver, A Piece of Cake, Upper High Street, February 2008

Proposals for a war memorial were widely discussed. Ultimately, the Green, east of the Whitehound pond, was obtained from Lord Bertie, and the memorial unveiled by Mr Lloyd George, then Prime Minister, on July 30th, 1921. The visit of the great War Minister naturally attracted an immense crowd, all anxious to see the statesman in the flesh, and, if possible, to shake hands with him at the reception.

The memorial, which was designed by the Surveyor of the Council, the late J T Robinson, took the form of a cross of Portland stone, 21 ft high, with names on a bronze tablet; it eventually cost £1,200

A History of Thame, J Howard Brown and William Guest

Jesse Matthews, War Memorial Garden, Upper High Street, July 2007

'It had been desired to include Whitehound pond in the (war) memorial by filling it in and making it into a garden; but it was thought to afford additional security in case of fire, and gave a 'rural aspect' to the town. The pond was, however, a source of danger; two horses had been rescued from it with difficulty; a pig had fallen through the ice in 1907 and had not been recovered for three or four days; in 1904, a boy of three had been drowned in it; further, it was alleged that the tarred roads so contaminated the water that horses would not drink it. Again, the pond was a constant source of expense, requiring periodic cleaning out as it became choked with filth; the last occasions had been in 1903 and 1915, when the cost was £18. Eventually it was filled in when the Pearce Memorial, a drinking fountain surrounded by a lily pond, was erected in 1926 by Ernest Pearce of Australia, as a monument to the late P H Pearce.'

A History of Thame, J Howard Brown and William Guest

Pearce Memorial, Memorial Gardens, Upper High Street, July 2007

The Star and Garter beer-house was first recorded in 1861 and described as being in Risborough Road. The name was derived from the Most Noble Order of the Garter. The Star forms part of the insignia and the use of the name celebrated allegiance to Queen Victoria who was head of the Order. The Wells family ran it as a beer-house from 1881 to 1953 and it only obtained a full licence when Hubert Brown took over the premises in 1953.

Thame-born Richard Walker has been landlord since 2006.

The Star and Garter is the only pub in Thame where Aunt Sally is played. This traditional game is played between two competing teams of eight players throwing batons at a wooden skittle about six inches tall known as a 'doll'. The doll stands on top of an iron two and a half feet above the ground, and each player has six batons ('sticks') which are two inches in diameter and eighteen inches long. Sticks are thrown from behind a line ten yards from the iron, and a point is only counted as long as the stick hits the doll cleanly before the iron. The competition is played over three 'legs' or 'horses' followed by a beer leg and the playing season takes advantage of the long summer evenings from May to September. The Star and Garter team competes in the South East Oxon League, Section II.

Richard Walker, The Star and Garter, Wellington Street, April 2008

Nick Newitt, Thame One Stop Centre, East Street, October 2007

John Markham (John the Stitcher), East Street, July 2007

The Cross Keys has imposed itself on the junction since New Road (now East Street) was built in the 1840s with Thomas Burnard as its first licensee.

The name can be associated with Christian heraldry, being a papal symbol and also the sign of St Peter, the gatekeeper of Heaven.

Of nearly eighty inns and ale-houses known to have existed in over sixty separate locations in the town and listed in *Thame Inns Discovered* only a dozen remain: The Six Bells, The Rising Sun, Birdcage, Abingdon Arms, The Spread Eagle Hotel, The Black Horse, Old Nag's Head, The Two Brewers, The Swan Hotel, The Star and Garter, The Cross Keys, and The Falcon.

The Cross Keys, Park Street, May 2008

Charles Hamer and the former Baptist Chapel, Park Street, April 2008

Park Street, November 2007

Park Street, December 2007

Tom Fletcher, Rosemary & Time, Park Street, August 2007

Park Street, May 2008

Thame Cycles, Park Street, August 2007

I started fishing when I was knee-high to my dad. Now I'm teaching fishing, and I get such a buzz out of talking to youngsters and introducing them to the sport. I've caught all the fish I ever want to catch, but if I can pass on to somebody else the techniques, just the little nuances of reading a river, of watercraft – if I can pass that on – then I get as big a buzz out of that as I do from actually fishing myself.

From a conversation with Ian Horrocks, November 2007

Ian Horrocks, Thame Tackle, Park Street, July 2007

My father, Ralph Seymour, opened up on the first of December 1960 doing all the British bikes at the time.

By the late 70s the British marques had all fallen by the wayside and he took on the agencies for Yamaha, Suzuki and Honda and we sold and worked on those until the early 1990s. When we gave up the agency for Suzuki, interest in the Classic British bikes was growing. He had raced a Mark VIII KTT Velocette with his own modifications until about 1952. The bike down in the showroom is one of a pair he built that were entered in a ten lap production race in the Isle of Man TT in the mid 70s. And because his main love was Velocettes we became Velo specialists.

When we were doing the Japanese bikes we came under a lot of pressure to adopt their corporate image but we didn't want to be the same as everybody else. We are still very similar to most motorbike dealerships of years ago. We have the stores upstairs, and as long as our MOT agency keeps running we can even carry on using the old fashioned Salter scales instead of a rolling road for brake testing. Now when people come in who haven't been here before you can see their mouths open, WOW! Look at this!

I first came here to help out because the storeman had left. I was waiting to go on to something else, but I just loved it so much I stayed. We don't need a computer other than the MOT one which we have to have. The stores, what's out in the stores, it's all in my head, I know what we've got.

Dad used to run an apprenticeship scheme. Towards the end of his days it was almost impossible to get anyone to take up a traditional apprenticeship. People seemed to want everything immediately and didn't seem to see the need to acquire the skills and knowledge an apprenticeship would give. It was almost like a cancer that crept in.

But I'm convinced that you've got to be really, really interested and involved in something to be able to build up your store of knowledge about it. And with the old bikes, as with old cars, you have got to have experience and knowledge of them and a certain amount of love for them: otherwise you're in the wrong business.

From a conversation with Liz Barrett, April 2008

Liz Barrett, R F Seymour Ltd., Motorcycle Engineers, Park Street, April 2008

Shell forecourt with Sainsbury's Local, Park Street, November 2007

AFTERWORD

to Leysis Quesada

Querida Leysis,

I linger over coffee in Rumsey's Chocolaterie considering these words. It's a sign of the times that the awning shading the window announces not only the name of the business but also the address of its website. When I first knew them, these premises were a family-run Grocer and Delicatessen: valued customers who were granted the privilege of a monthly account received handwritten statements. The table at which I sit is where the cheese counter used to be. Several years ago, Peter Jordan, who owned the business, asked me if I was going to photograph shopkeepers like himself, "Before we're all gone".

I remembered that earlier conversation when you proposed we both make photographs of our local towns and I began to make portraits of people I had got to know over the years. But your suggestion turned me into a traveller: I found myself becoming more curious, venturing into places I'd never previously visited, meeting new people. I also began creating a context for the portraits within both candid and consensual photographs in the street and direct representation of some of the architecture. Some of the photographs I showed you in Havana last year didn't make it into this final selection. Similarly there are others that you haven't seen before. Now I've arranged the whole sequence as if we were walking together through the town.

As I shuffled these random moments into a traceable geography I found things in the prints that I'd missed at the moment the shutter clicked: new mortar in old brickwork round a doorway, a third passer-by reflected in a window where before I'd only seen two, the plastic bag marked MONEY hanging from the vice in John the Stitcher's workshop. When I studied the portrait of Brian, the owner of the bookshop, I discovered the cover of the novel *Falling Man* by Don deLillo in the top left hand corner of the frame. DeLillo, in one of his other novels, has a photographer say to her reclusive subject: "Don't forget, from the moment your picture appears you'll be expected to look just like it." I love the idea, but don't worry; I know you won't entertain such an expectation of these photographs.

In the window of the Chocolaterie there is a framed photograph of the market. It was made, I learned, by the seamless joining of two old negatives. The content is plausible but if you know the place the resulting perspective is really disturbing. Other historical photographs hang inside, a view of sheep penned for market in temporary hurdles outside the Nag's Head, a view of the Upper High Street deserted except for a pony and trap. They offer glimpses into a former time just as these recent photographs continue that tradition and so invent another version of the past. The Upper High Street is recognisable in both, but even 100 parked cars gleaming in November sunlight do not – as yet – afford the same opportunities for wistful nostalgia as a solitary pony and trap.

As they accumulated I have shown prints to people who have viewed them through filters of local knowledge and acquaintance. You, however, cannot but help meet the page with your imagination free from any immediate associations. You and the traffic warden have no shared history! Perhaps you will look beyond the portraits and into the backgrounds. I wonder if you will focus on what we take for granted, the abundance and variety (sometimes even frivolity) of items in our shops. Jars of sun-dried tomatoes, chargrilled artichokes. The random jostle of plenty. Dog-chews, fishhooks, a rack of new tyres. The supermarket trolleys that have been filled and refilled, filled and refilled over and over again. In buying our few necessities we pass by so much that is made so easily available to us: I would not have imagined that shelves displaying mineral water would be stocked with a dozen brands, including one bottled in Fiji. Until, that is, I stopped and looked more closely. In the bookshop the Foreign Travel section prompts me to remember that while I may require a visa to enter your country I do not need permission to leave my own, as you in Cuba do.

The layout of the centre of the town remains almost unchanged since medieval times when one of the bishops of Lincoln laid out a new town centre and diverted the road from Oxford to Aylesbury to pass through his markets and increase their revenues.
I remember you commenting on the words *Scheduled Ancient Building Circa 1550* picked out on a timber-

framed building. They suggest an underlying historical security, a permanence upon which daily, monthly, yearly changes are written. This time last year that building was being renovated. It opened as a restaurant last November but is, I believe, already under new management. Enterprises come and go. People pass the CLOSING DOWN stickers for the last time, and Mi Casa's place is taken by a charity shop. Pied Pedaller, the toyshop, has finally closed and the building, formerly a cinema, is due to be demolished. A new library will be built on the site. Planning permission has been granted for a new livestock market just outside the town – the area it has occupied in North Street since 1951 will be redeveloped, though exactly how no-one is sure. Thame Tackle is in new ownership, and Craft 'T' Sue's has closed. A sign in the window announces TOY SHOP COMING HERE SOON. Gallery Hadley announces a 1/3 OFF SALE and the outside of the Old Nag's Head is being repainted: I make a new photograph.

The Round Table has held its Duck Race and the jeweller re-entered his shop. The braid cut for charity may even now be being worn as a wig by someone whose therapy cost them their hair, and the builders' skip has been hauled away. The dental practice has opened and the beer bottle been removed from the window ledge. A year has passed since those banner-wishes for a Happy 21st.

From halfway across the world the energy of a cyclone exhausts itself in a notice, in the photograph of a notice, in the Oxfam bookshop window.

Events slip away behind us, fugitive as a gesture, and I wonder what you will make of these pictures.

The man reading at the bus stop has gone upon his way: and a printer in Verona will bind my shadow into this book.

Hasta luego, John
8 August 2008

Acknowledgement

I wish to thank everyone I encountered while photographing: their generosity, patience, interest and assistance has made the preparation of this work both informative and enjoyable.

Books of specific local interest

A History of Thame, J Howard Brown B Sc (Lond) and William Guest MA (Oxon), F H Castle & Co, Thame, 1935

The Book of Thame, Gerald Clarke, Barracuda Books, 1978

An Innkeeper's Diary, John Fothergill, Chatto and Windus, 1931

My Three Inns, John Fothergill, Chatto and Windus, 1951

Thame Inns Discovered, Allan Hickman and David Bretherton, Daal Publishing, 2000

River Thame Old Chiltern's Son, Tony Chaplin, Tempus Publishing, 2007

Thame in Old Picture Postcards, Norman Waters, European Library, 1983

Thame Past and Present, Shaun Goffe, European Library, 1988

Changing Faces of Thame (Book One), Marilyn Yurdan, Robert Boyd Publications, 2006

Changing Faces of Thame (Book Two), Marilyn Yurdan, Robert Boyd Publications, 2007

John Hampden: The Patriot, 1594-1683, John Adair, Thorogood, 2003